Ph

Can it Really Rain Frogs?

John Malam

Contents

OXFORD UNIVERSITY PRESS

Introduction

Humans are curious by nature. We want to know the truth about things. That's the reason we ask questions. Historians and archeologists ask questions about the past. The police ask questions about how to solve crimes, and so on. By finding things out, we begin to understand the world. When scientists observe something in nature, they try to work out how it happens. Sometimes they do this by performing experiments.

However, no matter how hard we try, there are some things that cannot easily be explained. For example, is there life on other planets? This is one of the biggest questions in science, and no one has a definite answer to it yet. Other mysteries are much closer to home, as you'll find out in this book. Explanations can be given for some of them. But even though scientists have discovered reasons for why lots of things happen, there are still plenty of mysteries that remain unexplained.

Can you explain them?

Some of the mysteries we'll look at in this book are:

The Great Siberian Explosion

What could cause an explosion that could be heard 1200 kilometres away? (pages 4-7)

Oak Island pirate treasure

Why is it that advanced modern technology cannot reach this buried treasure? (pages 12-13)

Raining fish

Objects, animals and even people falling from the sky - did you know that some of these can be explained easily by the weather? (pages 16-19)

Atlantis

An ancient undersea city - could the legend of Atlantis be true? (pages 20-23)

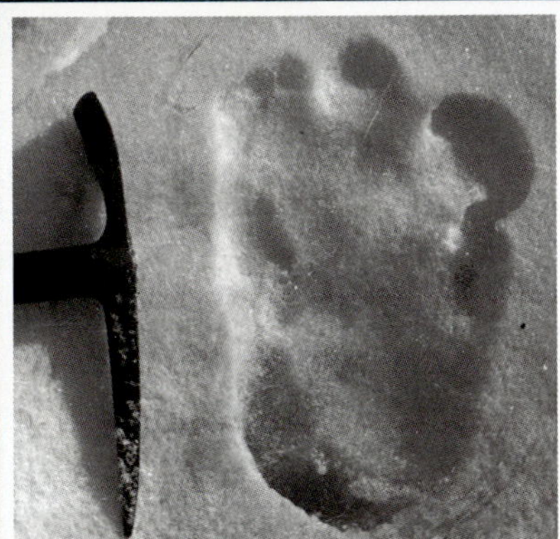

Big Foot

Giant, hairy, ape-like men - are the giant footprints that some people have 'discovered' just a hoax? (pages 30-33)

The Great Siberian Explosion

Early one morning in June, 1908, people living in Siberia, northern Russia, saw a bright light streak across the sky. It was just after 7 o'clock, and history was about to be made.

The streak, which looked like a long white scratch, grew until it seemed to have ripped the sky in two. Eyewitnesses said it was so bright it was almost impossible to look at. They said the sky seemed to be on fire. Whatever was making the line was on a high-speed collision course with Earth.

When? 30th June, 1908
Where? Tunguska, Siberia

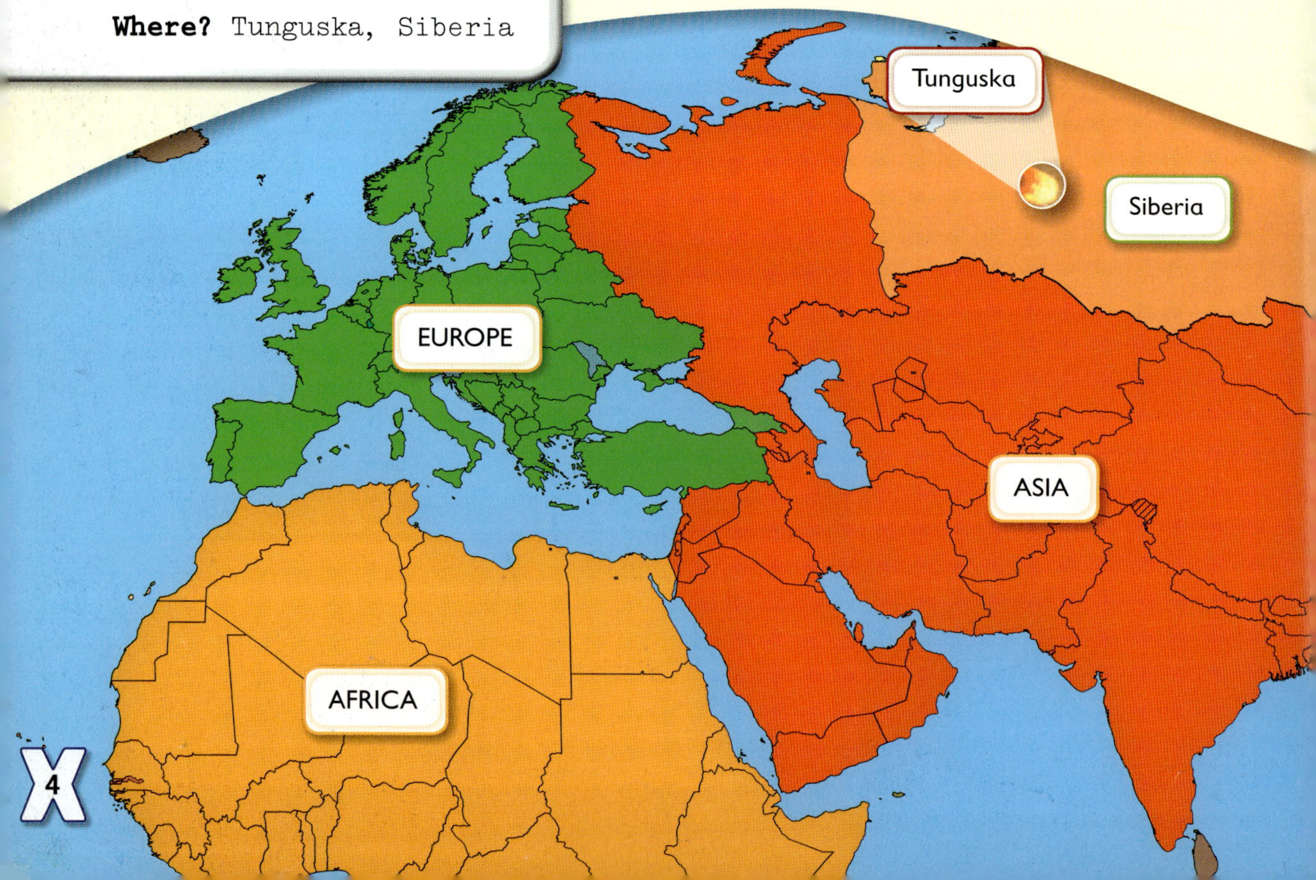

Tunguska
Siberia
EUROPE
ASIA
AFRICA

Kaboom!

The streaking object reached an area of Siberia called Tunguska and exploded. More than 300 kilometres away, villagers said they heard a booming noise as loud as thunder. It made their houses shake. Some people said they were knocked off their feet. A train driver who heard it thought he had crashed into something, so he stopped his train. He was 1200 kilometres away from the explosion.

Daylight nights

The explosion sent a giant cloud of dust high into the atmosphere. During the next few weeks, the dust had a weird effect on the night sky. Instead of it being dark at midnight, it was still light enough to read. Photographers took pictures of towns late at night. It looked as if they had been photographed in the daytime! There were 'daylight nights' in many countries of northern Europe during the summer of 1908. No one could explain why. It was a mystery.

Would the bright light have looked like this?

Examining the evidence

The blast had happened in one of the most remote places on Earth. It was almost twenty years before scientists found out about it and went to investigate. In 1927, a team of Russian scientists went to look, and they could hardly believe their eyes. Millions of trees had been knocked flat by the blast. The few trees still standing had been snapped in two, as if they were matchsticks. The blast zone stretched for as far as the eye could see. Something big – very big – had exploded here, but what?

Why did it happen?

THEORY 1 It was an atomic explosion

Why? The blast made a giant cloud shaped like a mushroom. An **atomic bomb** makes a mushroom cloud. The blast zone was massive. An atomic bomb destroys a vast area.
Why not? There were no signs of **radiation**. An atomic bomb leaves traces of radiation. Also the technology to build an atomic bomb had not yet been invented.
Conclusion: It was not caused by an atomic explosion.

THEORY 2 A UFO crashed into Earth

Why? An alien spaceship went out of control as it entered Earth's atmosphere and exploded.
Why not? Nothing from an alien spaceship has ever been found.
Conclusion: It was not caused by a **UFO**.

EXPLAINED

Researchers have tried to explain what happened at Tunguska. However, there is one theory that seems to be the most likely explanation – it was an explosion caused by a **meteoroid** (a 'shooting star') from space. A meteoroid is a lump of rock which sometimes hits the ground and leaves a deep, wide crater. However, this one exploded 5 to 10 kilometres above the ground, sending out a shock wave that flattened millions of trees.

Round and round in circles

When? since early summer, 1980
Where? Wiltshire, UK

Each summer, as fields of wheat and barley ripen in the sun, patterns of circles mysteriously appear in them. Some patterns are simple and have just one or two circles. Others are complicated and are made up of lots of circles. Have aliens landed in farmers' fields, or is someone playing a joke?

Crop circles: what we know

- Crop circles usually appear overnight.
- They can be any size, from 1 metre to 100 metres across or more.
- There are no trackways leading up to them across the fields.
- The stems of corn are all neatly bent over in the same direction.

Can you see how these crop circles were made?

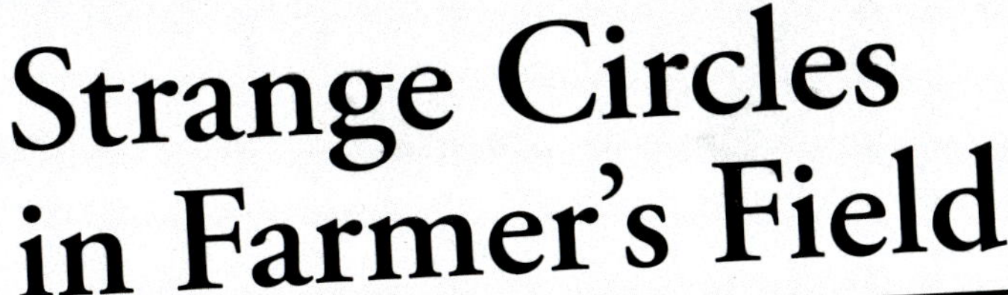

Strange Circles in Farmer's Field

May 1980
Wiltshire, England

A Wiltshire farmer has been puzzled by strange circles that have appeared overnight in his fields of wheat. The first circle measured 18 metres across, and since then more circles have appeared. "I put the first circle down to a freak gust of wind," the farmer said. "I ploughed it up and thought nothing more of it. There have been loads more since then. I don't know what's causing them."

Farmers are asked to contact the newspaper if they find circles in their fields.

Republic of Ireland

UK

Wiltshire

Did you know?

More crop circles have appeared in the English county of Wiltshire than anywhere else in the UK. Some of the first circles ever seen were spotted in Wiltshire, in the summer of 1980, and, since then, the county has become the world capital of cereology (the study of crop circles).

It's not the wind

At first, single circles were found on their own. Then, groups of circles were found arranged in patterns. The idea that the wind could make such precise patterns started to seem less likely. Therefore, if it wasn't the wind, it must be something else – but what?

People came up with lots of ideas to explain the causes of crop circles. These are some of the ideas – which would you believe?

- Blocks of ice falling from aeroplanes
- Humans having fun
- Giant hailstones
- Messages made by aliens trying to contact us
- Unknown energy forces, e.g. BOLS (balls of light)
- Whirlwinds
- Rabbits going round and round in circles
- The fields were 'remembering' where ancient circles of stone once stood (like Stonehenge)
- Unexploded bombs from World War II buried under the ground

Explaining the unexplained

All through the 1980s, circles kept cropping up in the fields of Wiltshire. Books were written about them and television programmes were made. Some TV crews even set their cameras to film at night, hoping to capture a circle being made, but they never did.

Then, in September 1991, Doug Bower and Dave Chorley said the circles were a practical joke made by them. They said they had made their first circle in 1980. Since then, they had made hundreds more. Doug and Dave sneaked into fields at night, carefully walking along wheel tracks made by tractors. Then, they used wooden boards to flatten the crop into a circle. After an hour they were finished, and home they went, leaving the circle to be 'discovered' the next day.

Doug Bower (left) and Dave Chorley (right), making crop circles.

EXPLAINED

Not everyone believed Doug and Dave's story. So many circles had been made, they could not have been behind them all. Perhaps there were other practical jokers at work at the same time, but they've never been found out. For some people, crop circles are still unexplained. What do you think?

The Money Pit

Canada

Nova Scotia

Oak Island

When? 1795 to now

Where? Oak Island, Nova Scotia, Canada

Is pirate treasure buried at the bottom of a pit on an island off the coast of Canada? Treasure hunters have been digging up Oak Island for 200 years, but there's still no sign of any treasure.

1

In 1795, three boys find a dip in the ground at the foot of an oak tree. It looks like a pit that has been filled in. There is a block and tackle hanging from a branch above the dip.

2

The boys think the block and tackle have been used to lower something heavy into the pit. They decide that pirates have buried treasure there ...

3

They start digging. They come to a layer of stones. The treasure must be under them. It isn't. They carry on digging. Now they find a layer of logs. Then two more layers of logs. They give up when they have dug 10 metres.

4

The story of the Oak Island treasure spreads. In 1804, a team digs down to 27 metres, through logs and charcoal that have been put there on purpose. It must be valuable treasure if someone has taken this much trouble to hide it.

5

Tunnels join the pit to the sea, and when the team disturbs the tunnels, water pours in. The pit floods.

6

More teams try their luck. Each time they have to pump water out of the flooded pit. Drilling machines reach down to 50 metres. They still find no treasure.

7

In 1971, the pit is 72 metres deep. A television camera is sent down and seems to film chests. The pictures are very fuzzy. They might not be chests. Soon after, the sides of the pit collapse.

UNEXPLAINED

The search continues. It is the biggest and longest treasure hunt in history. One thing is for certain – the Money Pit has cost more money than it's ever given up!

Bright lights at night

Unexplained lights at night have led to many stories. The strange lights have been blamed on top-secret spy planes, UFOs and even fairies. One type of mystery light is known as 'fairy fire' because, in the past, people thought it was made by fairies. In the myths of Britain, fairy fire was blamed on Robin Goodfellow, a mischievous hobgoblin (a type of fairy).

Robin Goodfellow and fairy fire – a traditional tale

One night, some men were walking home across a lonely heath. Before long, they had lost their way. A hobgoblin called Robin Goodfellow lived on the heath. He watched the men as they struggled to find their way in the dark. He was a naughty imp who played tricks on humans, and he went up to the men and said, "Follow me, and I will show you the way off the heath."

The men thought he had come to their rescue, so they set off after him. But Robin Goodfellow was no ordinary hobgoblin. He was a shape-shifter and could change his shape into whatever he wished. He turned himself into a will-o'-the-wisp – a strange, flickering light that covered him from head to toe. The men could not take their eyes off this fairy fire. They were under Robin Goodfellow's spell, and he led them up hills, down ditches and through puddles and mud.

Only when the first rays of sunlight broke through the darkness was the spell lifted, and Robin Goodfellow sent the men on their way with the sound of his laughter ringing in their ears.

His other name

Robin Goodfellow is a character in old stories from Britain. For example, in the 1600s, William Shakespeare wrote about him in his famous play *A Midsummer Night's Dream*. In the play, Shakespeare called him Puck.

EXPLAINED

What is fairy fire?

At night, balls of light can sometimes be seen glowing low over swamps and marshes. They are known as fairy fire, will-o'-the-wisp, elf fire, jack-o'-lantern and walking fire. These weird lights are probably caused when natural gas from rotting vegetation escapes from under the ground and briefly catches fire.

What goes up, must come down

Have you heard anyone say, "It's raining cats and dogs"? It's a strange saying. People obviously do not mean that cats and dogs really are dropping out of the sky, even though that is what it seems to mean. However, some very unusual things have fallen from the sky ...

Bread dough UNEXPLAINED

When? 1992

Where? Bellingham, Washington, USA

What happened? A 9 kg ball of bread dough crashed on to the roof of a house.

Worms UNEXPLAINED

When? 2007

Where? Jennings, Louisiana, USA

What happened? Blobs of worms landed in a street.

Frogs EXPLAINED (SEE PAGE 19)

When? 1973

Where? Brignoles, France

What happened? Thousands of toads dropped onto a village.

Blood UNEXPLAINED

When? 1551

Where? Lisbon, Portugal

What happened? It rained blood.

Fish

EXPLAINED

(SEE PAGE 18)

When? 1859

Where? Mountain Ash, Wales, UK

What happened? Hundreds of little fish fell out of the sky.

Sand

EXPLAINED

(SEE PAGE 19)

When? 2008

Where? Milford Haven, Wales, UK

What happened? Sand from the Sahara Desert in Africa fell on towns in south Wales.

Money

UNEXPLAINED

When? 1940

Where? Meshehera, Russia

What happened? Silver coins fell during a storm.

People

EXPLAINED

(SEE PAGE 19)

When? 1930

Where? Rhön Mountains, Germany

What happened? Five glider pilots crashed to the ground inside giant hailstones.

Cans and bottles

UNEXPLAINED

When? 1974

Where? Hamilton, New Zealand

What happened? It rained cans and bottles for four hours.

Turn the page to find out why strange things might fall from the sky.

Why do fish fall from the sky?

There was great excitement when hundreds of tiny fish fell on Mountain Ash, Wales, 1859. A few were sent to the British Museum, London. At the museum, Dr Gray, a fish expert, said they were fish from a local stream. He said that someone must have scooped them up in a bucket of water, then thrown the water up in the air, and that is how the fish had dropped out of the sky. Dr Gray thought someone had played a practical joke – but he might have been wrong.

'Fish rain' has fallen hundreds of times. It has happened all over the world and has got nothing to do with people throwing water. Instead, it is to do with the weather. In stormy weather, strong winds can blow water from rivers and lakes into the air. That is how fish find themselves up in the sky.

What about the other things?

It is not only fish that get lifted up by the wind. Falls of frogs and sand can be explained as the result of stormy weather. Sometimes they only get blown a short distance, but sand from the Sahara Desert can travel thousands of kilometres before it falls to the ground inside raindrops.

Five glider pilots became human hailstones and fell from the sky over Germany in 1930. Their story is also linked to the weather. They flew into a storm and had to jump from their gliders. As they parachuted down, strong winds blew them back up into the clouds time and again. Each time they went up, they were coated in a new layer of ice. Eventually, with so much ice on their bodies, they were too heavy to stay inside the clouds, and they came to the ground as 'human hailstones'.

Atlantis – the long lost island

About 2400 years ago, there was a famous writer in ancient Greece called Plato. In his books he described a large island called Atlantis. Ever since Plato wrote about it, people have tried to find Atlantis. The lost island of Atlantis is one of the world's greatest mysteries - but is it fact or fiction?

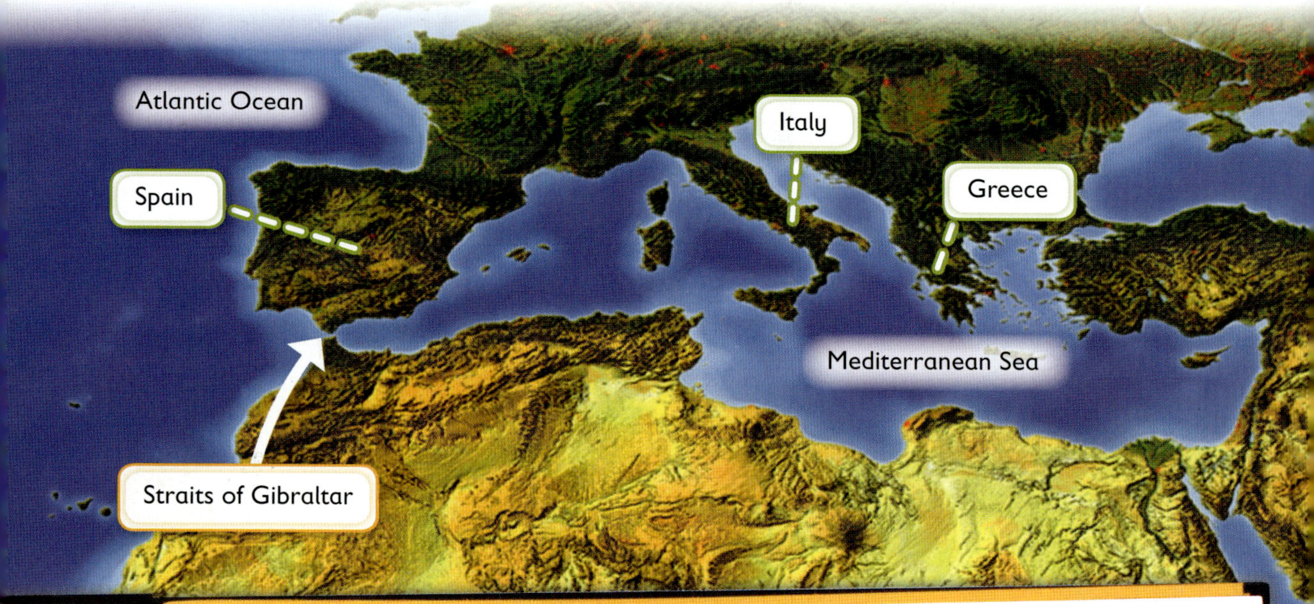

Atlantic Ocean
Spain
Italy
Greece
Mediterranean Sea
Straits of Gibraltar

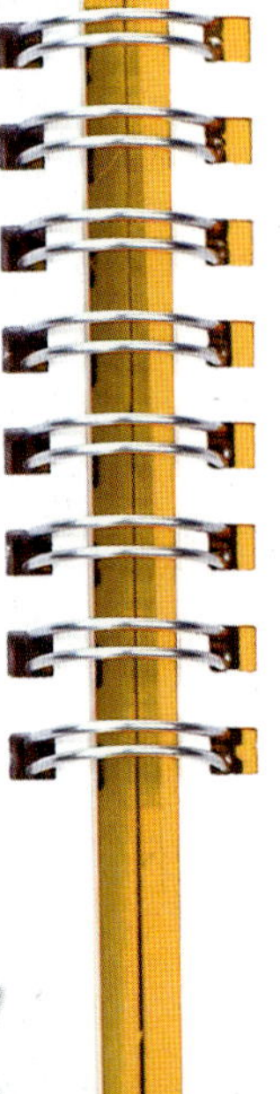

Atlantis according to Plato

What Plato said	Meaning
Atlantis was beyond the **Pillars of Hercules**.	Atlantis was in the Atlantic Ocean. The Pillars of Hercules are found at the Straits of Gibraltar, the narrow piece of water that separates the Atlantic Ocean from the Mediterranean Sea.
Atlantis was about 555 kilometres long and about 370 kilometres wide.	Atlantis was the world's tenth biggest island – a little smaller than the island of Britain.
Atlantis was a great power, 9600 years before the time of Solon (a famous lawmaker in the city of Athens).	Atlantis was a powerful city about 11 600 years ago.
Atlantis was suddenly destroyed by earthquakes and floods. It sank overnight.	Atlantis was destroyed because of a natural disaster.

A description of Atlantis

Plato said the Atlanteans (the people who lived on Atlantis) lived in a great city. The city was circle-shaped and about 18 kilometres across. It was made from a series of rings, each one separated from the next by a ring of water. Tunnels joined the rings of land together, and that's how the Atlanteans moved from one ring to the next. Inside the city were magnificent buildings, whose walls were covered with gold and silver. Beyond the city was a vast plain, on which there were many villages.

How did Plato know about Atlantis?

Plato never saw Atlantis. If it had ever existed, it had disappeared long before he lived. In Plato's own time people thought that Atlantis was real. They told stories about it, and it is from these that Plato got the information for his books. If Plato had not written about Atlantis, we might not know about the island at all. But what is the real story? Has there ever been an island like the one described by Plato?

Turn over to find out more about the long lost island of Atlantis.

Atlantis – fact or fiction?

As the centuries passed, people changed their minds about Atlantis. No one took Plato's description of a lost island seriously anymore – they said it was a made-up story. That was until 1882, when Ignatius Donnelly, an American writer, wrote a book about Atlantis. It had some daring ideas in it. Donnelly's biggest idea was about the destruction of Atlantis. He said perhaps Plato had got this bit of the story right - that long ago a real island had been destroyed by earthquakes and floods. But where was it? The search began to find a place that could have been Atlantis.

Researchers have argued that Atlantis could be in one of many areas all over the world. Here are a few of the places.

EXPLAINED

Is Santorini Atlantis?

There is one place that seems more likely than anywhere else to be the home of the Atlantis story. It's the Greek island of Santorini, which is in the **Aegean Sea**. **Archaeologists** have found traces of an ancient civilization that lived there, which they call Minoan. The Minoans lived on Santorini 4500 years ago, until their beautiful island was almost completely destroyed by a giant volcano, 3600 years ago.

By the time of Plato, 1200 years after the eruption, all that was left of the Minoans and their island were vague memories. Stories about them were passed from generation to generation. Like all stories, bits were added to make them more exciting, such as saying the lost island was far away from Greece. But, at the heart of the stories, was something we now know was true – an island really was destroyed by natural forces, and a civilization was wiped out, just as Plato said. So, the island of Santorini might be Atlantis.

A scene showing the Minoans in daily life.

Expedition Everest

When? 8th June, 1924
Where? Mount Everest, on the border of Nepal and Tibet

George Mallory and Andrew Irvine wanted to be the first people to climb Mount Everest, the world's highest mountain (8848 metres high). Whether they did or not, is the greatest unexplained mountaineering mystery of all time.

George Mallory

Born: 18th June, 1886
Died: 8th June, 1924
Age at death: 37
Place of birth: Mobberley, Cheshire
Nickname: 'Sir Galahad'

Andrew Irvine

Born: 8th April, 1902
Died: 8th June, 1924
Age at death: 22
Place of birth: Birkenhead, Merseyside
Nickname: 'Sandy'

Climb of their lives

- The climb began at the end of March, 1924. The plan was to set up camps along the route, rest for a while, then continue to the top.
- Camp Six was the last of the camps, set up on 3rd June. It was 8170 metres up the mountain, about 678 metres from the **summit**.
- At 8 am on 8th June, Mallory and Irvine set off from Camp Six.
- At 12:50 pm, Mallory and Irvine were seen high on the mountain, slowly climbing towards the summit. This was the last time they were seen alive.

UNEXPLAINED

Two mysteries

Mallory and Irvine died on Mount Everest on 8th June, 1924. No one knew how they died or if they had reached the summit. Some people thought they had reached the top, but there was no way to prove it.

Did they or didn't they reach the summit?

In 1999, seventy five years after Mallory and Irvine disappeared, an expedition set out to find their frozen bodies. Mallory's body was found on 1st May, but there was no sign of Irvine. It looked as if Mallory had died from a fall, and one mystery was finally solved. But, the biggest mystery still remained – had he reached the top of Mount Everest? Mallory had taken a photograph of his wife with him. His plan was to leave it on the summit. His pockets were checked, but there was no sign of the photograph. Could the missing photograph be a clue that he had reached the top? Or did it slip from his pocket as he fell?

The plaques commemorating the two climbers.

The lost flyer

When? 2nd July, 1937
Where? Pacific Ocean

In 1920, Amelia Earhart had her first ride in an aeroplane. The flight lasted ten minutes, and it changed her life. From then on she knew she wanted to learn to fly planes – she wanted to be a pilot.

Amelia Earhart	
Born	24th July, 1897
Died	Unknown; went missing 2nd July, 1937
Age at death	39
Place of birth	Atchison, Kansas, USA
Nickname	'Meeley' or 'Millie'

1 **3rd January, 1921**
Amelia has her first flying lesson. It is in a biplane – a plane with two wings, one above the other.

2 **June, 1921**
Amelia buys her first plane – a biplane painted bright yellow. She calls it 'The Canary', after the yellow songbird.

3 **22nd October, 1922**
Amelia sets a world record for a woman pilot when she flies 'The Canary' 4300 metres above the ground.

4 **18th June, 1928**
Amelia becomes the first woman to fly across the Atlantic Ocean. She is a passenger. The flight lasts 20 hours and 40 minutes.

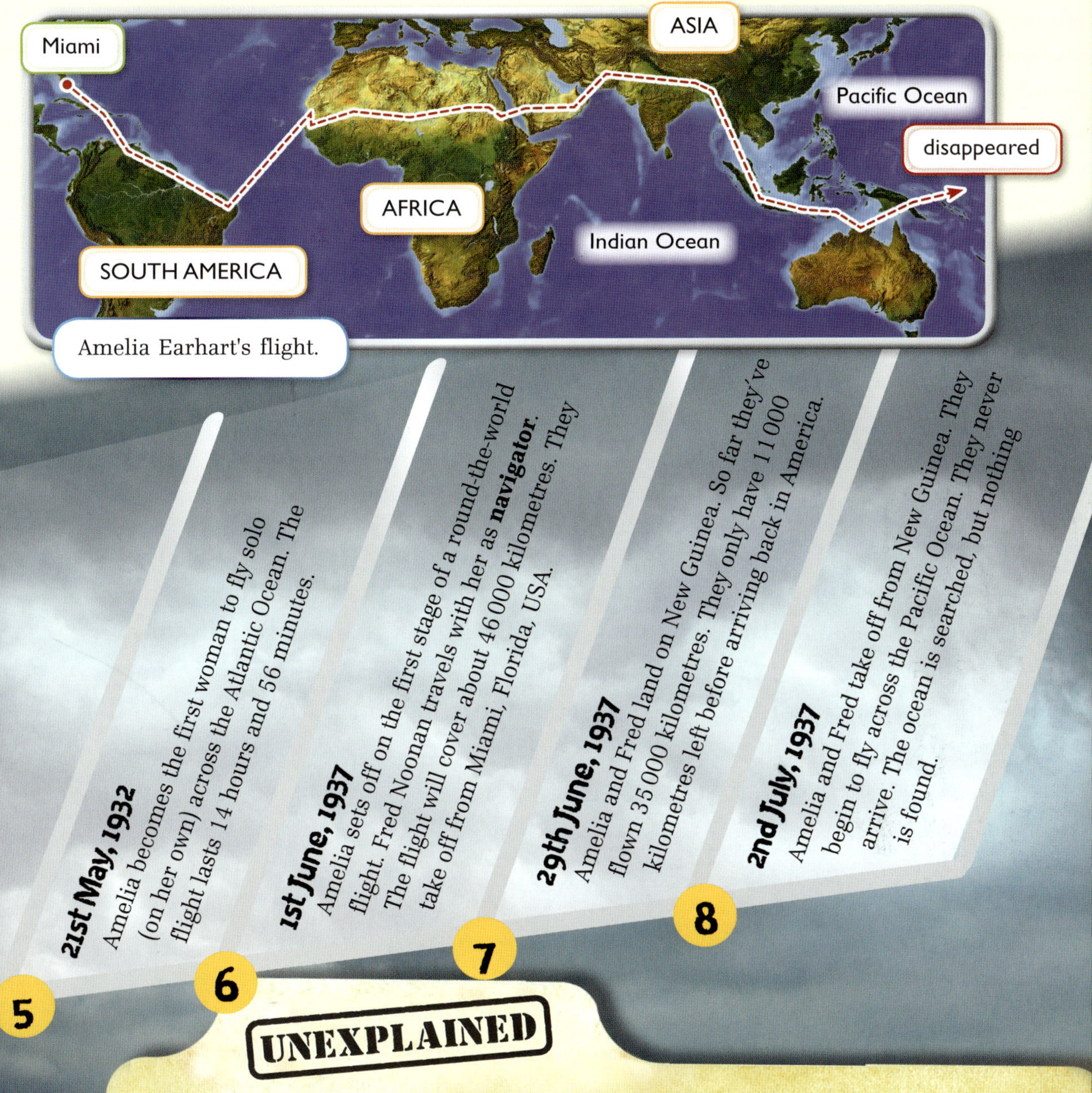

Amelia Earhart's flight.

5 **21st May, 1932**
Amelia becomes the first woman to fly solo (on her own) across the Atlantic Ocean. The flight lasts 14 hours and 56 minutes.

6 **1st June, 1937**
Amelia sets off on the first stage of a round-the-world flight. Fred Noonan travels with her as **navigator**. The flight will cover about 46 000 kilometres. They take off from Miami, Florida, USA.

7 **29th June, 1937**
Amelia and Fred land on New Guinea. So far they've flown 35 000 kilometres. They only have 11 000 kilometres left before arriving back in America.

8 **2nd July, 1937**
Amelia and Fred take off from New Guinea. They begin to fly across the Pacific Ocean. They never arrive. The ocean is searched, but nothing is found.

UNEXPLAINED

What went wrong?

There are lots of ideas to explain what happened to Amelia Earhart and Fred Noonan. These are the two most popular ideas:

- The plane ran out of fuel, crashed into the sea and sank.
- The plane was off course and landed on an **uninhabited** island, where Amelia and Fred eventually died.

What do you think?

Shergar, the kidnapped racehorse

When? 8th February, 1983
Where? Newbridge, Co.Kildare
Republic of Ireland

Why would anyone kidnap a horse? That is what happened to Shergar, a famous racehorse that vanished without trace in1983.

Winning streak

Shergar started racing in 1981. He did well and won lots of races. Soon, people were saying he was good enough to win that year's Epsom Derby, one of the biggest horse races in the world. The race took place on 4th June, 1981, and Shergar was the favourite to win. At the halfway point he was in third place. Then, with about 600 metres to go, Shergar took the lead and raced home to win. He finished about 24 metres in front of the horse in second place – a record distance that has never been broken.

Shergar	
Born	1978
Last seen	8th February, 1983
Colour	**Bay**
Place of birth	Republic of Ireland
Number of races	8
Number of wins	6
Most famous win	Epsom Derby, 1981
Winnings	£436 000

Shergar in a race. He is thought by many people to be the best racehorse that ever lived.

Shergar Kidnapped!

8th February 1983

The champion racehorse, Shergar, has been stolen from the farm where he lives. Witnesses claimed to have seen a gang of six men drive off with him in a horsebox earlier today. The police have been informed and are searching the area.

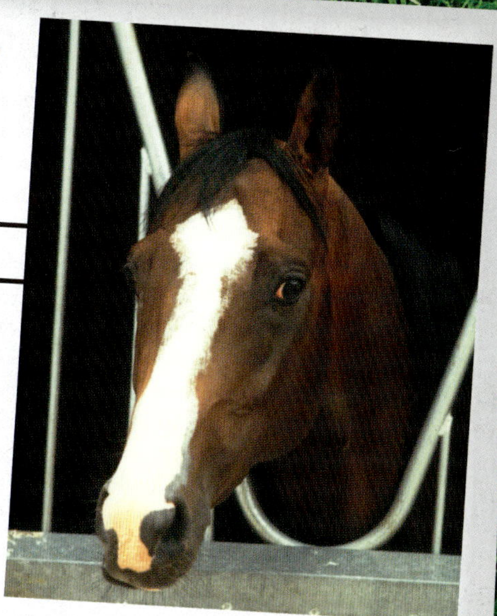

Who took Shergar and why?

Soon after the kidnap, the gang holding Shergar got in touch with his owners and demanded money. Shergar would be freed if the money was paid. The owners refused to pay, and Shergar was never seen again. No one has ever owned up to taking Shergar. Over the years, there were rumours that Shergar had been seen. It is now believed that he was killed soon after he was taken and his body buried in a field.

Perhaps one day someone who knows what happened will tell the truth. Until then, the story of Shergar the kidnapped horse remains an unexplained mystery.

How much?

Shergar's owners have never said how much ransom money the kidnappers asked for, but some people think it was £5 million!

What's big and hairy?

When? 20th October, 1967
Where? Bluff Creek, California, USA

In parts of Canada and the USA, native peoples tell stories about an unexplained animal that lives in the woods. There are many names for the creature. Some people call it Sasquatch, others prefer Bigfoot. No matter what it is called, one thing is clear – the mysterious animal is big and hairy!

USA
California

Bigfoot

Other name	Sasquatch
Sasquatch means	'Wild Man'
Posture	Walks upright on two legs
Appearance	Covered head to toe in long, shaggy, dark fur
Height	2 to 2.5 metres tall

Bigfoot timeline

Date	Place	Event
1811	USA	An explorer found a giant footprint, 35 centimetres long.
1884	Canada	A newspaper said a Bigfoot had been caught.
1924	USA	A group of miners said they were attacked by several Bigfoot creatures.
1928	Canada	A hunter said a Bigfoot carried him to its den.
1967	USA	A woodcutter said he watched three Bigfoot creatures looking for food.
1967	USA	Roger Patterson and Robert Gimlin claimed they filmed a Bigfoot.
1988	USA	A boy out fishing said a Bigfoot watched him.
1996	USA	A man and his wife said a limping Bigfoot surprised them.
2006	Canada	A woman said she spotted a Bigfoot at the edge of a forest.

Caught on film

In 1967, Roger Patterson and Robert Gimlin claimed they had seen a Bigfoot in California, USA. Even more amazing, the men had caught the creature on film. They filmed it for less than a minute, and their incredible pictures caused a sensation. Had they seen a giant ape, totally new to science? Or had they filmed an ordinary man in a gorilla costume? From the day it was made, the Patterson-Gimlin film has been the subject of debate. For some people it is proof that Bigfoot exists. For others, it is no more than a **hoax**.

Bigfoot seems to have a relative on the other side of the world. It is another big, hairy animal, but this one does not live in forests. The tallest mountains in the world are in Nepal and Tibet, and it is amongst the snow-capped Himalayas where a mysterious, secretive animal is said to live. It is called the Yeti.

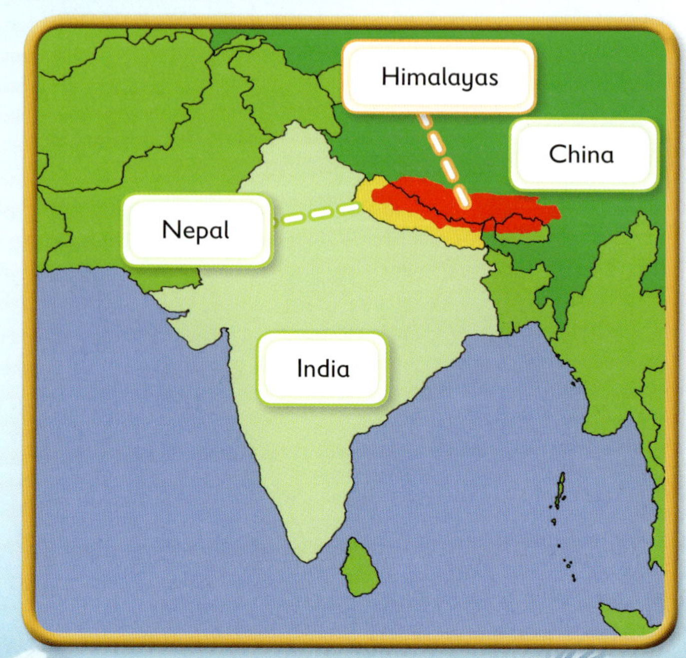

Yeti

Other name	Abominable Snowman
Yeti means	'Rocky Place Bear'
Posture	Walks upright on two legs
Appearance	Covered head to toe in long, shaggy, dark fur
Height	2 to 2.5 metres tall

Yeti timeline

Date	Place	Event
1832	Nepal	A report said local people were scared of a hairy, wild man.
1889	Nepal	Giant footprints were found in the snow.
1921	Nepal	Climbers said they spotted a group of large, dark creatures.
1951	Nepal	Giant footprints were found in the snow and photographed.
1954	Nepal	A British newspaper claimed a **monastery** had a Yeti **scalp**.
1984	Nepal	A climber said he was followed by a large, furry creature.
2007	Nepal	Giant footprints were found, each one 33 centimetres long.

UNEXPLAINED

Can the Yeti be explained?

If there really is such an animal as the Yeti, it certainly knows how to hide itself away. Local people believe in it, as do many visitors who claim to have seen it. Or have they? What if they have confused it with another animal? Bears live in the Himalayas, and that is what some Yeti sightings might actually be. Footprints in the snow could be hoaxes made by people playing practical jokes.

Did you know?

According to people in Nepal, the best way to escape from a Yeti is to run downhill. If it chases after you, it will trip over its long fur and fall over!

Have you seen an ABC?

ABC stands for Alien Big Cat. Despite the name, it has got nothing to do with aliens from space. In this case, the word 'alien' means an animal that is found living in the wild, far away from its natural home. ABCs are pumas and leopards that might be roaming the British countryside.

Big cats in Britain

Big cats have been spotted roaming all over Britain. Many sightings can be explained as:

- hoaxes (practical jokes)
- mistaken identity (not cats at all)
- feral cats (escaped domestic cats living wild).

Big cats versus tame cats

	Puma	Leopard	Domestic cat
Height	70 centimetres	90 centimetres	23 centimetres
Length	1 to 2 metres	1 to 2 metres	50 to 70 centimetres
Weight	30 to 70 kilograms	30 to 70 kilograms	4 to 7 kilograms
Natural home	North America, South America	Africa, Asia	Worldwide

Exmoor covers a total of 691 square kilometres, so there are plenty of places for an ABC to hide!

The Beast of Exmoor

Exmoor is a National Park in south-west England. It's a large open area of hilly **moorland**, and since the 1970s people have reported seeing big cats there.

In 1983, a farmer said his flock of sheep had been attacked by an unidentified big cat. Some of the sheep were killed. The government decided something had to be done, and soldiers were sent to Exmoor with orders to shoot to kill. But the soldiers saw nothing, and no shots were fired.

Newspapers reported the story and called the mysterious cat the 'Beast of Exmoor'. One newspaper offered a reward to the person who captured or killed the animal, but no one ever succeeded.

Feedback

THE EXMOOR ADVERTISER

To the editor

People argue about whether big cats are living amongst us. There are many reasons to believe that they are.

There have been big cat sightings for many years. Farmers say their sheep have been attacked. There is even evidence that some sheep were killed. What else could have done this? Even the government took these claims seriously. They sent soldiers to Exmoor.

Big cats may have been brought into the country as illegal pets. Then they have escaped or been set free into the countryside.

Some people have argued that big cat sightings are a hoax. Others say that the big cats could be large domestic cats. They ask why big cats have not been caught.

However, sightings of native wild cats are rare. Wild cats and big cats are shy creatures. If they do not exist, why do we continue to hear of sightings?

Big cats are alive and well and roaming the British countryside.

Rudy Jones

Bodmin, UK

What do you think?

The Beast of Bodmin

Bodmin Moor is in Cornwall, south-west England. A big cat might be on the prowl amongst the moor's grassy hills and boulders. It was first spotted in the 1970s, and occasional sightings are still made today. It is described as looking like a black panther or a dark coloured mountain lion, with large yellow eyes. It hisses and growls, just as a panther does. In 1998, a large black cat, about one metre long, was filmed on the moor – it could be an over-grown domestic cat, or a new type of wild cat.

EXPLAINED

Strange but true

In 1995, a cat skull was found on Bodmin Moor. It was bigger than a domestic cat's skull, and for a time it looked as though the mystery of the Beast of Bodmin had been solved. The skull was sent to the Natural History Museum, London, where it was examined by an expert in cat bones. She identified it as the skull of a leopard - but there was more. Inside the skull was an egg case laid by a cockroach. It was a type of cockroach that doesn't live in Britain. Therefore, it showed that the leopard had not died in Britain and the skull had been brought into the country. It may have been thrown away on Bodmin Moor to trick people into thinking it belonged to the mysterious big cat!

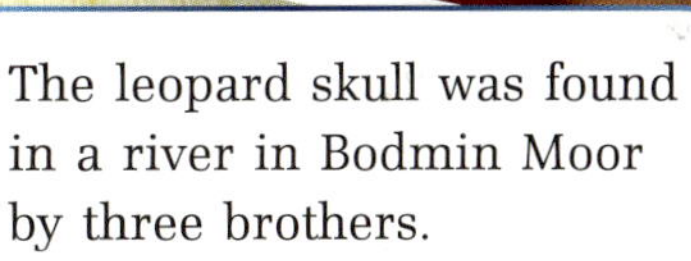

The leopard skull was found in a river in Bodmin Moor by three brothers.

The truth really is out there

People are fascinated by unexplained mysteries. There is something about them that grabs our attention and makes us want to try to work them out. Somewhere, somehow, most mysteries can probably be explained. The more we search for answers, the greater the chances are of finding out the truth.

Odd ones out

Many of the world's mysteries have a number of possible explanations. But some people still refuse to believe them. For them, the truth is still waiting to be found. For example, even though many people believe that crop circles are the work of hoaxers, a few people are convinced they're made by space aliens. What do you think?

Can you solve a mystery?

Remember, the best way to solve a mystery is by asking questions. The more you ask, the more you learn, until all the pieces of the puzzle fall into place. The truth is out there somewhere – you've just got to find it.

Glossary

Aegean Sea	part of the Mediterranean Sea which lies between Greece and Turkey
archaeologist	a person who studies human history and prehistory
atomic bomb	a bomb which uses powerful energy to destroy things
bay	a horse that has a reddish-brown body, a black mane and tail and black lower legs
hoax	a joke to trick people into believing something that isn't true
meteoroid	a small body that moves through space. If it enters Earth's atmosphere it becomes a meteorite
monastery	a place where monks or nuns live, work and pray
moorland	an area of high land in its natural state, which is not used for farming or other uses
navigator	a person who directs the route of a journey using instruments and maps
Pillars of Hercules	the name given to two large rocks on either side of the Straits of Gibraltar which legend says were forced apart by a strong man called Hercules
radiation	a type of energy which can be dangerous to people's health and the environment
scalp	skin on top of the head
summit	the top of a hill or mountain
UFO	Unidentified Flying Object. An object seen in the sky, which cannot be explained by science
uninhabited	an area where no people or animals live

Index